WITHDRAWN

WORLD OF
MAMMALS

SQUIRRELS

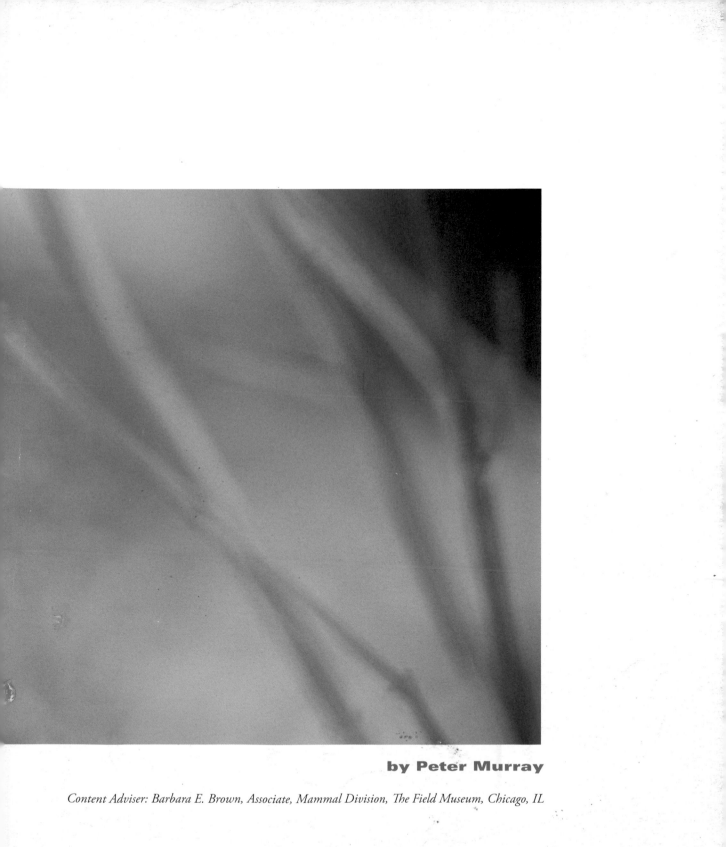

by Peter Murray

Content Adviser: Barbara E. Brown, Associate, Mammal Division, The Field Museum, Chicago, IL

THE CHILD'S WORLD®, CHANHASSEN, MINNESOTA

SQUIRRELS

Published in the United States of America by The Child's World®
PO Box 326 • Chanhassen, MN 55317-0326 • 800-599-READ • www.childsworld.com

Acknowledgements:

The Child's World®: Mary Berendes, Publishing Director

Editorial Directions, Inc.: E. Russell Primm, Editorial Director; Pam Rosenberg, Editor;
Judith Shiffer, Assistant Editor; Matt Messbarger, Editorial Assistant; Susan Hindman,
Copy Editor; Emily Dolbear, Proofreader; Judith Frisbie and Olivia Nellums, Fact
Checkers; Tim Griffin/IndexServ, Indexer; Cian Loughlin O'Day, Photo Researcher,
Linda S. Koutris, Photo Editor

The Design Lab: Kathleen Petelinsek, Designer, Production Artist, and Cartographer

Photos:

Cover/frontispiece: Niall Benvie/Corbis; half title/CIP: Corbis.

Interior: Animals Animals/Earth Scenes: 5-top left and 8 (Joanne Muemoeller), 5-middle
left and 22 (Zigmund Leszczynski), 16 (Manoj Shah), 21 (Fred Whitehead), 27 (Gerlach
Nature Photography), 35 (Breck P. Kent); Gary W. Carter/Corbis: 5-bottom left and 34,
25; Digital Vision: 5-top right and 15, 29, 36; Getty Images: 13 (Stone/Mervyn Reese);
Joe McDonald/Corbis: 19, 32; Photodisc: 5-bottom right and 30, 10.

Library of Congress Cataloging-in-Publication Data

Murray, Peter, 1952 Sept. 29–
  Squirrels / by Peter Murray.
    p. cm. — (The world of mammals)
  Includes index.
  ISBN 1-59296-503-2 (lib. bdg. : alk. paper) 1. Squirrels—Juvenile literature. I. Title.
II. World of mammals (Chanhassen, Minn.)
  QL737.R68M776 2005
  599.36—dc22   2005000536

TABLE OF CONTENTS

Chapter One

Squirrelly Behavior

One day, I was watching a gray squirrel trying to get onto my bird feeder. First it tried to climb the metal post. But it couldn't get past the metal disk I had installed on the post to keep squirrels off. I laughed. I was way too smart for that beady-eyed, bushy-tailed, seed stealer! The squirrel then climbed halfway up the trunk of a nearby tree and launched itself at the feeder. It missed, crashing to the ground. I laughed again as it shook itself off and ran back to the tree.

A few minutes later, I looked out the window and saw the squirrel hanging by its hind legs from the tip of a branch about 3 meters (10 feet) above the feeder. After thinking about it for about ten seconds, the squirrel let go and dropped. Again, it missed the feeder.

"Stupid squirrel," I said to myself with a superior smile.

Sometime later, I glanced out the window to find that same squirrel sitting on the feeder, looking very fat and happy, munching my sunflower seeds. How did he get there?

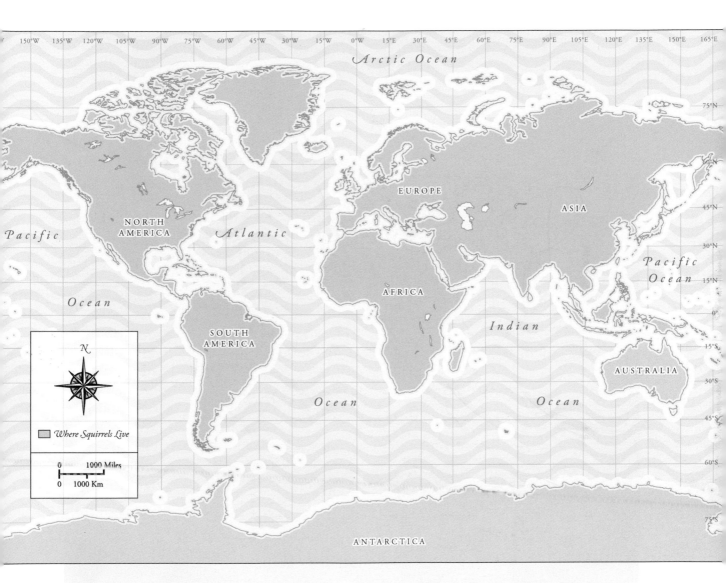

I still don't know. But I'm going through a lot more seed these days.

The same thing can happen to bird feeders in less urban, more heavily wooded areas. Only the creatures

Squirrels can be found almost everywhere on Earth. Antarctica and Australia are the only two continents without any squirrel species.

A Douglas squirrel feasts on the seed in a birdfeeder.

eating the sunflower seeds might not be what you'd expect. Not mice. Not rats. Not raccoons. Not even typical squirrels. Would you believe flying squirrels? It's true! These pale-brown creatures, not much larger than chipmunks—with bulging black eyes and soft, wispy tails—simply glide to a feeder from nearby trees.

When most of us think of squirrels, we think of the bushy-tailed, tree-climbing, nut-eating gray ones that live in city parks, backyards, and wooded areas throughout most of North America and Europe. And if you live where there are trees, you probably have squirrels for neighbors. Even without trees, the squirrel family does just fine. In the Arizona desert, for example, rock squirrels, a type of large ground squirrel, go after bird feeders. So does the Harris's antelope squirrel, another type of ground squirrel.

There are more than 267 **species** in the squirrel family, including tree squirrels, ground squirrels, prairie dogs, flying squirrels, chipmunks, and marmots. Squirrels live on every continent except Australia and Antarctica. They can be found in the driest deserts, in tropical rain forests, and on the Arctic tundra. They are one of the most common and familiar wild mammals on our planet—and one of the most fun to watch.

Chapter Two

What Is a Squirrel?

What do squirrels have in common with mice, beavers, and porcupines? They are all rodents.

About forty percent of all mammal species are rodents, from mice weighing less than 6 grams (0.21 ounce) to

Porcupines are rodents that have quills. These are a kind of hair that detaches easily. A porcupine's attacker will find out just how painful it can be to have quills stuck in its body!

the capybara, a South American rodent the size of a large dog. Rodents can be found grazing in grassy fields, **burrowing** deep beneath the earth, scampering through the treetops, swimming the lakes and streams, and sailing through the air. The first rodents appeared about 50 million years ago. The first squirrels appeared about 35 million years ago.

But what makes a rodent a rodent? They have hair, they give birth to live young, and they feed their young milk. But so do elephants, kangaroos, and other mammals. Rodents are mostly small—there are no elephant-size rodents. But there are many small mammals that are not rodents, such as weasels and shrews. All rodents eat plant matter. But so do deer, giraffes, and cattle. What makes a rodent a rodent are its amazing teeth.

TEETH

Incisors are the chisel-shaped front teeth—humans have four on the top and four on the bottom—that you use when you bite a chunk out of an apple. Rodents also use their incisors—two on the top and two on the bottom—to bite into apples

and other things. Beavers chew through trees. The house mouse can use its incisors to cut through the plaster walls of your home. Fox squirrels easily slice through the hull of the toughest nut, and mole rats use their enormous incisors to dig tunnels through dirt and sand.

Rodent incisors are longer, stronger, and sharper than those of other mammals. But what really makes them different is that they are constantly growing. In fact, a rodent must use its incisors every day to wear them down. If it doesn't, they will soon grow too long for its mouth.

You might think that all that chewing would make the incisors dull, but they are made to stay sharp. The front of the incisor is coated with a thin, hard layer of **enamel.** The rest of the tooth is made of dentin, a softer material. As the animal gnaws, the dentin wears away faster, leaving a knifelike edge of enamel. Rodents' incisors get sharper as they chew. These sharp teeth and powerful jaws mean that squirrels and other rodents can eat many kinds of foods, including the hardest nuts and the inner bark of trees.

All rodents have sharp, powerful incisors. But what makes squirrels differ-

Would You Believe?
The name *rodent* comes from the Latin word *rodere,* which means "to gnaw."

Would You Believe?
The word *squirrel* comes from the ancient Greek word *skiouros,* or "shade-tail."

ent from mice, porcupines, rats, and other rodents?

What's the first thing you notice when you see a gray squirrel? Its big, bushy tail.

TAILS

We humans don't have tails, so we don't often think about how useful a tail can be. When we go out in the rain, we use an umbrella or a raincoat to keep the rain off our heads. The gray squirrel uses its tail. It also uses its tail to shade itself from the hot sun.

When we lose our balance, we flail our arms wildly and often fall down. The squirrel uses its tail for balance. That's how they are able to scamper along utility wires without falling.

Gnawing on hard foods such as nuts and tree bark helps squirrels keep their teeth sharp and short.

13

But even squirrels take a fall every so often. Their tails come in handy then, too. A falling squirrel will spread its legs and stretch out its tail to create air resistance. This slows the squirrel down enough so that it doesn't land too hard. When the squirrel hits the ground, it usually recovers quickly and runs straight back up the tree trunk.

The squirrel's tail is handy in cold weather, when it works like a huge furry scarf. Squirrels also use their tails like signal flags, letting other squirrels know when they are angry, frightened, or curious.

Most ground squirrels do not have large bushy tails. Prairie dog tails are downright stumpy. But they still use their tails to "talk" to each other. With a complex system of tail wags, body language, and more than a dozen different calls, prairie dogs are the squirrel family's most expert communicators. Some experts think that prairie dog "language" is as complex as that of dolphins.

Would You Believe?
Once, a Mexican tree squirrel leaped from a cliff and landed on a ledge 180 meters (590 ft) below. The squirrel got up and hopped off, apparently unhurt.

Prairie dogs don't have the long, bushy tails that people usually picture when they think of squirrels, but they are a kind of squirrel.

FEET

Running full speed up and down tree trunks is probably not something you do every day, but for tree squirrels it is a way of life. Tree trunks and limbs are squirrel highways. Watching a pair of squirrels chasing each other around a tree trunk, you might wonder what happened to the law of gravity. Up, down, sideways—it doesn't seem to matter. The squirrels stick to the tree like Velcro.

Their secret is in their long, flexible toes, and their sharp, curved claws. A squirrel has four toes on each front

A five-striped palm squirrel runs headfirst down a tree in India.

foot and five toes on each of its hind feet. A squirrel's foot can grab just about any surface—any tiny crack or knob or crevice is enough to give the squirrel a grip. Gray squirrels can climb any tree, as well as drainpipes and brick walls.

SENSES

The life of a squirrel might look like fun, but it isn't always easy. Food can be scarce at times, and there are always larger animals that think a plump squirrel would make a fine meal. All squirrels have to keep a sharp eye out for **predators.** Fortunately, squirrels have excellent eyesight. Their eyes are very large and set far apart. They are positioned on their heads so that they can see in front of them, to either side, and even above.

Do you ever smell your food before you taste it? So do squirrels. Smell is their most important sense when it comes to deciding what's for dinner. A squirrel can tell a good nut from a bad nut just by giving it a sniff. Their sense of smell is so good, a squirrel can find a nut it has buried even when it is covered by lots of snow.

Smell is also important for squirrel communication. Squirrels **mark** their territory with urine. The strong smell tells other squirrels to stay away! Squirrels also have oil **glands** on their paws that leave scent markers on tree branches. Females leave these scent markers so that male squirrels can find them when it is time to **mate.**

FUR

Squirrels and other rodents usually have fur that helps them hide from predators. Ground squirrels are usually light brown and gray, the color of the dirt and grasses where they live. Red squirrels are a rusty-brown color, much like the pine trees and pinecones of their native woods. Gray squirrels are the color of hardwood tree trunks—a squirrel hanging to the side of a tree can be almost invisible if it is not moving.

Not all gray squirrels are gray. Some gray squirrels are born black. This color variation is called **melanism.** Black squirrels are found in many places in the eastern United States. There are also gray squirrels that are white. Pure white animals with red eyes are called albinos.

Would You Believe?
In the town of Olney, Illinois, albino squirrels are given the right-of-way on the town's streets. Anyone who accidentally hits a white squirrel can be fined twenty-five dollars. Olney is home to more than 200 albino squirrels.

Chapter Three

Making a Living

Squirrels are one of the most successful mammal families on Earth, but finding food, avoiding predators, and making baby squirrels are dangerous and difficult jobs. A gray squirrel that is both smart and lucky might live to the ripe old

An Eastern gray squirrel looks out of a tree hole.

age of ten—but most don't make it through their first year. Most of a squirrel's life is spent searching for food. Fortunately, squirrels eat just about anything. The gray squirrel's diet includes nuts, acorns, seeds, corn, berries, mushrooms, and the soft inner bark of trees. Most of the squirrel's diet is vegetarian, but they also eat insects, discarded deer antlers, eggs, baby birds, and small mammals.

Many ground squirrels also eat just about anything they can grab. The thirteen-striped ground squirrel eats seeds, fruits, nuts, flowers, and other vegetable matter—but about half of its diet is grasshoppers, beetles, worms, caterpillars, mice, baby birds, and even each other!

HOARDING

Have you ever heard the expression "to squirrel something away"? It means to hide something you might need in the future. Squirrels have long been admired for their ability to store large quantities of food.

Gray squirrels bury acorns one at a time. During the late summer and fall, a squirrel might bury several hundred nuts. Later, when there is snow on the ground and food is scarce, the squirrel will find the buried acorns by using its keen sense of smell.

Would You Believe?
Prairie dogs are one of the few members of the squirrel family to feed mostly on grass. Grass makes up about two-thirds of their diet. A single prairie dog can eat about 1 kilogram (2 pounds) of grass a week. They also eat green leafy plants, seeds, and the occasional insect.

But even the hungriest squirrel won't find every single acorn it buried. Many of the acorns will stay in the ground until spring, then sprout to become new oak trees.

Red squirrels also hoard food, but they don't bury it one nut at a time. Red squirrels build **larders,** where they store large numbers of pinecones. They also store mushrooms,

A red squirrel eats a spruce cone. Red squirrels store pinecones in underground larders.

A bobcat prepares to eat its latest catch—a gray squirrel.

which they first dry by sticking them on tree branches for a few days.

Fox squirrels, flying squirrels, and ground squirrels also hoard large quantities of nuts and seeds. Ground squirrels build underground larders that can hold enough food to get them all the way through winter.

STAYING ALIVE

Most squirrels do not live longer than one or two years. Many animals—including <u>human</u> beings—like to eat squirrels. <u>Hawks</u>, <u>snakes</u>, <u>bobcats</u>, <u>pine martens</u>, <u>foxes</u>, <u>coyotes</u>, <u>wolves</u>, and many other predators prey on squirrels. Automobiles also kill large numbers of squirrels.

A squirrel's best defense is its speed and alertness. When threatened, tree squirrels seek safety in trees. Ground squirrels hide in their burrows. Flying squirrels avoid most predators by being active only at night and by gliding from tree to tree to escape danger.

FAMILY LIFE

Most squirrels are active all winter long. When the weather gets extremely cold, a squirrel might spend several days sleeping in its nest. But before long, it will be out again, **foraging** for food. In the late winter and early spring, squirrels become very active. You will often see gray squirrels chasing each other up and down tree trunks and leaping from branch to branch. It looks as if they are playing—but those squirrels are engaged in serious business. They are searching for a mate.

When the days first start to get longer, female squirrels leave a scent that attracts males. Several males often pursue a single female, fighting with each other and chasing the female from tree to tree. When the most powerful male has chased off his rivals, he mates with the female. About six weeks later, the female gives birth.

Gray squirrels usually have two or three young at a time. The baby squirrels are born hairless and blind. A baby flying squirrel weighs only about 6 grams (0.21 oz). Baby gray squirrels weigh about 14 grams (0.5 oz).

Squirrels, like all rodents, grow quickly. Within two months, the squirrels have left their nest and are finding their own food. By the following winter, the young female squirrels are ready to raise their own families.

If you found a nest of baby squirrels, you might not realize that they were squirrels. Babies are born without hair so they don't look like adult squirrels.

Chapter Four

Squirrel Types

TREE SQUIRRELS

There are eight species of tree squirrel in North America. The most common and familiar is the gray squirrel of the eastern United States. The largest is the fox squirrel, which can weigh as much as 1.5 kilograms (3.5 lbs). Other North American species include the western gray squirrel, Abert's squirrel, and the small but aggressive red squirrel.

Tree squirrels are also common in Europe, Africa, and Asia. The giant squirrels of India and southeast Asia are up to 0.5 meter (20 in) long, with another 0.5 meter of tail! Giant squirrels come in a variety of colors. Some are dark red, while others are black with yellow stripes on their faces. They are often found on banana plantations. Giant squirrels live much longer than their smaller cousins. In captivity, a giant squirrel can live for more than twenty years.

Would You Believe?
The long-nosed squirrel of Southeast Asia eats mostly ants, termites, and earthworms.

GROUND SQUIRRELS

The ground squirrels include a wide variety of species, from the smallest chipmunk to the yellow-bellied marmot, which can measure 0.8 meters (31.5 in) long including the tail.

The thirteen-striped ground squirrel,

An Eastern chipmunk, its cheeks full of food, peeks out from a hole in a tree.

found throughout the central United States and Canada, is commonly seen on golf courses and in other open areas. In some places, they have become serious pests on farms. The golden-mantled ground squirrel of the western United States is often seen in campgrounds. Dozens of similar species inhabit just about every part of North America.

PRAIRIE DOGS

Prairie dogs are found in the middle West, from Montana down through Texas and northern Mexico. We don't usually think of prairie dogs as squirrels, but they are a type of ground squirrel. What makes them different from other squirrel family members is their diet of grass and leaves, their stumpy tails, and the fact that they live in underground burrows that are part of large colonies.

Would You Believe?
In 1900, a prairie dog town larger than many states was discovered in Texas. The town was about 400 kilometers (250 miles) long and 160 kilometers (100 mi) wide, with a population of about 400 million.

MARMOTS

Marmots are large ground squirrels that live in the northern United States and Canada. They are also common throughout northern Asia and in the mountainous areas of Europe.

Prairie dogs live in family groups called coteries. A coterie is usually made up of one male, one to four females, and their offspring under the age of two.

Marmots live in underground burrows. Some species live in colonies and dig large networks of tunnels. Marmots

The hoary marmot sends out a shrill alarm whistle when it senses danger and wants to warn other colony members. This is why they are sometimes called whistlers.

are quite a bit larger than other ground squirrels—the yellow-bellied marmot can weigh as much as 5 kilograms (11 lbs).

Groundhogs—also called woodchucks—are a type of marmot common in the eastern and midwestern United States. You might not think a groundhog is related to the familiar gray squirrel—but if you startle a groundhog near a tree, it might just scamper up that trunk. Although they prefer to stay on the ground, groundhogs are expert climbers.

CHIPMUNKS

These small, fast-moving ground squirrels have striped faces and backs and weigh 30 to 150 grams (1 to 5 oz). There are more than twenty species of chipmunk in North America, but it takes an expert to tell them all apart. Like most other squirrels, chipmunks will eat just about anything they can find or catch.

During the fall, chipmunks store large quantities of food. They have large pouches in their cheeks that they use to carry food back to their underground nests. Sometimes

A southern flying squirrel takes flight. They can glide through the air for more than 50 meters (164 ft).

a chipmunk will stuff its cheek pouches so full that it looks like it has an enormous, lumpy head.

FLYING SQUIRRELS

Flying squirrels sail through the air by stretching out a flap of skin that runs from their hind legs to their front legs. The skin catches the air like a kite, and they use their flattened tails to steer. Flying squirrels do not actually fly, but they can glide for more than 50 meters (164 ft).

There are two species of flying squirrel in North America—the southern flying squirrel and its larger cousin, the northern flying squirrel. Flying squirrels are quite common wherever there are wooded areas. Unlike other squirrels, most flying squirrels are nocturnal—they are only active at night and so are not often seen.

Asia is home to about thirty-three species of flying squirrel, including the giant flying squirrels of Southeast Asia, which can grow to more than 1 meter (3 ft) in total length. These squirrels are considered a delicacy in Taiwan, where they are hunted for their meat.

Would You Believe?
One of the strangest of all squirrels is the rare woolly flying squirrel. Covered with a thick layer of soft, woolly fur, this squirrel lives high on the rocky slopes of the Himalaya mountains in Pakistan. At 1.2 meters (3.9 ft) from its nose to the tip of its tail, the woolly flying squirrel is the longest member of the squirrel family.

Chapter Five

Squirrels and People

When the first European explorers reached the eastern coast of North America, they found a dense, endless hardwood forest. The forest was rich in walnut, hickory, hazelnut, oak, and other nut trees. The forest floors were loaded with berries, mushrooms, and seeds. It is said that in those days, a squirrel could have started at the Atlantic Ocean and hopped from tree branch to tree branch, never stopping to touch the ground, all the way to the Mississippi River.

In the north and far west were tens of millions of acres of pine trees with

The Delmarva Peninsula fox squirrel is on the U.S. endangered species list, but recovery efforts are helping to increase the animal's population.

Much of the northeastern United States was once covered by pine forests such as this spruce forest in Maine's Acadia National Park.

*Much of the hardwood forest in the United States
has been cut down to create farmland.*

their nutritious pinecones—favorite foods of red squirrels, Abert's squirrels, and Douglas squirrels. To the west, more than 2.5 million square kilometers (1 million sq mi) of grasslands supported huge numbers of ground squirrels and prairie dogs.

No one knows how many squirrels once lived in North America, but it was certainly more than we have today. The number of prairie dogs alone may have been in the billions.

Today, most of the hardwood forests of North America have been converted to farms, roads, and cities. There are probably fewer tree squirrels than there once were, and there are far fewer prairie dogs. But squirrels have been surviving for tens of millions of years, and they have learned to survive in our city parks, our golf courses, our farms, and in our backyards. No matter where you live, squirrels are your neighbors.

Glossary

burrowing (BUR-oh-ing) digging a hole or tunneling underground

enamel (ih-NAM-uhl) the substance that makes up the hard, white surface of teeth

foraging (FOR-ij-ing) the act of searching for food

glands (GLANDZ) body parts that produce certain substances or allow substances to exit the body

larders (LAR-durz) storage places for food; pantries

mark (MARK) the act of using smells or other substances to set the limits, or boundaries, of one's territory

mate (MAYT) the act of a male and female animal coming together to produce offspring

melanism (MEL-uh-niz-uhm) an increased amount of black pigment in the hair, skin, or feathers of a living thing

predators (PRED-uh-turz) animals that hunt other animals for food

species (SPEE-sheez) a group of animals that share certain characteristics

For More Information

Read It

Jacobs, Lee. *Squirrels*. San Diego: Blackbirch Press, 2002.

Jango-Cohen, Judith. *Flying Squirrels*. Minneapolis: Lerner Publications, 2004.

Schaeffer, Lola. *Squirrels*. Chicago: Heinemann Library, 2004.

Look It Up

Visit our home page for lots of links about squirrels:
http://www.childsworld.com/links

Note to Parents, Teachers, and Librarians: We routinely verify our Web links to make sure they are safe, active sites—so encourage your readers to check them out!

The Animal Kingdom
Where Do Squirrels Fit In?

Kingdom: Animal

Phylum: Chordates (animals with backbones)

Class: Mammalia (mammals)

Order: Rodentia (rodents)

Family: Sciuridae (squirrel family)

Index

About the Author

Peter Murray has written more than 80 children's books on science, nature, history, and other topics. An animal lover, Pete lives in Golden Valley, Minnesota, in a house with one woman, two poodles, several dozen spiders, thousands of microscopic dust mites, and an occasional mouse.